# THE TRUTH ABOUT INDEPENDENCE DAY

## CHARLOTTE TAYLOR

Please visit our website, www.enslow.com. For a free color catalog of all our high-quality books, call toll free 1-800-398-2504 or fax 1-877-980-4454.

**Library of Congress Cataloging-in-Publication Data**
Names: Taylor, Charlotte, 1978- author.
Title: The truth about Independence Day / Charlotte Taylor.
Description: New York : Enslow Publishing, 2023. | Series: The truth about early American history | Title from cover. | Includes bibliographical references and index.
Identifiers: LCCN 2022000281 (print) | LCCN 2022000282 (ebook) | ISBN 9781978527843 (library binding) | ISBN 9781978527829 (paperback) | ISBN 9781978527836 (set) | ISBN 9781978527850 (ebook)
Subjects: LCSH: Fourth of July–Juvenile literature.
Classification: LCC E286 .T39 2023 (print) | LCC E286 (ebook) | DDC 394.2634–dc23/eng/20220105
LC record available at https://lccn.loc.gov/2022000281
LC ebook record available at https://lccn.loc.gov/2022000282

Published in 2023 by
**Enslow Publishing**
29 E. 21st Street
New York, NY 10010

Copyright © 2023 Enslow Publishing

Portions of this work were originally authored by Katie Kawa and published as *The Declaration of Independence Wasn't Signed on July 4th: Exposing Myths About Independence Day*. All new material in this edition was authored by Charlotte Taylor.

Designer: Rachel Rising
Editor: Megan Quick

Photo credits: Cover, Artimages / Alamy Stock Photo; Cover, pp. 1-6, 8-10, 12, 14-16, 18, 20, 22-24, 26-28, 30-32 pashabo/Shutterstock.com; Cover, pp. 1-6, 8-10, 12, 14-16, 18, 20, 22-24, 26-28, 30-32 orangeberry/Shutterstock.com; Cover, pp. 1-6, 8-10, 12, 14-16, 18, 20, 22-24, 26-28, 30-32 iulias/Shutterstock.com; Cover, Brian A Jackson/Shutterstock.com; Cover, pp. 1, 3, 5, 6, 9, 10, 12, 15, 18, 20, 23, 24, 27, 28, 30-32 Epifantsev/Shutterstock.com; p. 4 Dmytro Balkhovitin/Shutterstock.com; p. 5 Ollyy/Shutterstock.com; p. 7 https://commons.wikimedia.org/wiki/File:Map_of_territorial_growth_1775.svg; p. 8 https://commons.wikimedia.org/wiki/File:Writing_the_Declaration_of_Independence_1776_cph.3g09904.jpg; p. 9 Photo © Christie's Images / Bridgeman Images; p. 11 Illman Brothers, and John Trumbull/Libary of Congress; p. 13 Wangkun Jia/Shutterstock.com; p. 14 Everett Collection/Shutterstock.com; p. 15 https://commons.wikimedia.org/wiki/File:Gilbert_Stuart_Williamstown_Portrait_of_George_Washington.jpg; p.17 Joseph Sohm/Shutterstock.com; p. 19 https://commons.wikimedia.org/wiki/File:Johannes_Adam_Simon_Oertel_Pulling_Down_the_Statue_of_King_George_III,_N.Y.C._ca._1859.jpg; p. 21 Artindo/Shutterstock.com; p. 21 https://en.wikipedia.org/wiki/File:King_George_III_of_England_by_Johann_Zoffany.jpg; p. 22 Sean Pavone/Shutterstock.com; p. 23 https://commons.wikimedia.org/wiki/File:The_Bell%27s_First_Note_by_JLG_Ferris.jpg; p. 25 sirtravelalot/Shutterstock.com; p. 26 https://commons.wikimedia.org/wiki/File:JohnAdams.png; p. 27 https://commons.wikimedia.org/wiki/File:Mather_Brown_-_Thomas_Jefferson_-_Google_Art_Project.jpg; p. 29 gary718/Shutterstock.com.

All rights reserved. No part of this book may be reproduced in any form without permission in writing from the publisher, except by a reviewer.
Printed in the United States of America

Some of the images in this book illustrate individuals who are models. The depictions do not imply actual situations or events.

CPSIA compliance information: Batch #CSENS23: For further information contact Enslow Publishing, New York, New York, at 1-800-398-2504.

Find us on

# CONTENTS

THE FACTS ABOUT THE FOURTH ............. 4
FIRST STEPS TO FREEDOM .................... 6
SIGNING THEIR NAMES ...................... 10
WHERE WAS WASHINGTON? .................. 14
MADE FOR THE MOVIES ..................... 16
PARTY IN THE COLONIES ................... 18
THE KING AND THE DIARY .................. 20
THE SOUND OF FREEDOM ................... 22
AMERICA CELEBRATES ...................... 24
FRIENDS AND FOES ......................... 26
OUR TRUE HISTORY ........................ 28
GLOSSARY ................................. 30
FOR MORE INFORMATION .................. 31
INDEX .................................... 32

# THE FACTS ABOUT THE FOURTH

Flags waving, fireworks booming, and all things red, white, and blue: in the United States, we **celebrate** the Fourth of July in a big way. Many people think it marks the day the Founding Fathers signed the **Declaration** of Independence, right? Not so fast.

Fireworks have been part of Independence Day since its first anniversary in 1777.

July 4, 1776, is an important day in American history. But that might not be for the reasons you think. Sometimes stories change over time, and facts get twisted around. Getting those facts straight is the best way to understand the true story of the United States and the road to independence.

### EXPLORE MORE!

THE POPULATION OF AMERICA HAS GROWN A LOT SINCE 1776. THAT YEAR, THERE WERE ABOUT 2.5 MILLION PEOPLE LIVING IN THE 13 COLONIES. BY 2021, THE POPULATION WAS A LITTLE OVER 330 MILLION. THAT'S MORE THAN 130 TIMES LARGER THAN WHEN IT BEGAN.

# FIRST STEPS TO FREEDOM

The 13 original colonies were founded by Great Britain starting in the early 1600s. But by the 1760s, the colonists were unhappy with British rule. The problems just kept getting worse. Finally, the Continental Congress—a group of men sent from most of the colonies—voted to declare independence from Britain on July 2, 1776. This was part of the Lee Resolution, a set of **proposals** made by Richard Henry Lee.

It was two days later, on July 4, when the Continental Congress **approved** the wording of the Declaration of Independence. It **formally** stated the reasons why the colonies were breaking away from Britain.

## Explore More!

THE CONTINENTAL CONGRESS FIRST MET IN 1774. IN THE BEGINNING, MOST PEOPLE DID NOT WANT TO BREAK FREE FROM GREAT BRITAIN. THEY WANTED THE COLONISTS TO HAVE MORE RIGHTS AND FREEDOMS. BUT THEY ALSO WANTED TO REMAIN BRITISH CITIZENS.

A group of five men had the job of writing the Declaration of Independence. Thomas Jefferson wrote the original **draft**. The group also included Benjamin Franklin and John Adams. They made some changes to it, as did the Continental Congress. The final resolution was adopted on July 2. Adams, who would

This painting shows, left to right, Benjamin Franklin, John Adams, and Thomas Jefferson at work writing the Declaration of Independence.

become the second president of the United States, believed this would be the day Americans would remember. He wrote, "The Second Day of July 1776 . . . will be celebrated as the great anniversary Festival."

As it turned out, Adams was right about Americans having a big celebration in July. He was just two days off!

## EXPLORE MORE!

THE DECLARATION OF INDEPENDENCE INCLUDES A LONG LIST OF REASONS WHY THE COLONISTS WERE UNHAPPY WITH BRITISH RULE. THEY PAID TAXES THAT THEY THOUGHT WERE UNFAIR. THE KING, GEORGE III, WOULDN'T ACCEPT MANY OF THE COLONIES' LAWS. AMERICANS THOUGHT THE KING SHOULD NOT HOLD SO MUCH POWER OVER THEM.

# SIGNING THEIR NAMES

The Declaration of Independence was approved by most colonies on July 4. You might think that the **document** was also signed on this date. However, the New York **delegates** didn't even approve it until July 15. And the document still needed to go to the printer.

The Declaration of Independence started as a handwritten draft. Late on July 4, 1776, the Congress sent it to a printer named John Dunlap. He printed about 200 paper copies of the document. These were sent to people throughout the new states. None of these was the copy that was signed by the Continental Congress delegates.

## EXPLORE MORE!

ONLY 26 COPIES OF THE DECLARATION OF INDEPENDENCE THAT WERE MADE BY JOHN DUNLOP IN JULY 1776 ARE STILL AROUND TODAY. GEORGE WASHINGTON READ ONE COPY TO HIS TROOPS IN NEW YORK CITY. IT IS IN POOR CONDITION, BUT IT STILL EXISTS.

This painting shows Thomas Jefferson presenting the first draft of the Declaration of Independence to the Continental Congress.

In late July 1776, the Declaration of Independence was rewritten by hand. A man named Timothy Matlack spent about two weeks carefully writing it on parchment, a special animal skin prepared for that purpose. This is called an **engrossed** copy. That is the copy that the delegates signed.

According to official records, the Declaration of Independence was signed by most of the delegates of the Continental Congress on August 2, 1776. Some delegates signed even later than that. The names of the 56 signers weren't shown to the public until January 1777.

## EXPLORE MORE!

THE BEGINNING OF THE DECLARATION OF INDEPENDENCE IS THE MOST WELL-KNOWN PART, STATING "ALL MEN ARE CREATED EQUAL" AND THAT THEIR RIGHTS INCLUDE "LIFE, LIBERTY, AND THE PURSUIT OF HAPPINESS." THESE WORDS WERE MEANT TO **INSPIRE** COLONISTS WHO WERE UNSURE IF IT WAS WISE TO SEPARATE FROM BRITAIN.

The Declaration of Independence was signed by most delegates in this room in Philadelphia, Pennsylvania.

# WHERE WAS WASHINGTON?

George Washington was a major figure in America's fight for freedom from Britain. But most of his work in those early years was on the battlefield. In spite of what many people think, Washington did not sign the Declaration of Independence.

John Hancock signs the Declaration of Independence. Today, people still say "put your John Hancock on it" if they want someone to sign something.

In the summer of 1776, George Washington was busy leading the Continental army. He was in New York with his troops. Washington would become the first American president. However, the president of the Continental Congress at the time was John Hancock. He signed the document first. It's easy to spot his name because he wrote it so large!

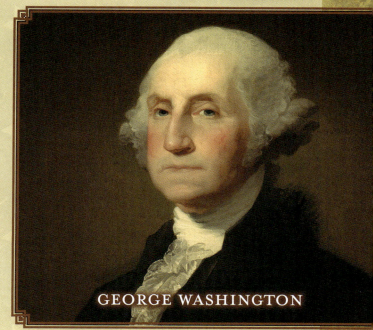

GEORGE WASHINGTON

## EXPLORE MORE!

BY THE TIME THE DECLARATION OF INDEPENDENCE WAS SIGNED, THE **AMERICAN REVOLUTION** HAD BEEN GOING ON FOR MORE THAN A YEAR. IT BEGAN ON APRIL 19, 1775, WITH SHOTS FIRED IN LEXINGTON, MASSACHUSETTS. THE COLONISTS WOULD NOT BE TRULY FREE FROM BRITAIN UNTIL THE WAR ENDED IN 1783.

# MADE FOR THE MOVIES

Sometimes movies or TV shows make up things about history. This happened with the Declaration of Independence. A 2004 movie called *National Treasure* suggested that there was a map or secret code on the back of the document. This would be exciting, but it is not true.

That doesn't mean the back of the Declaration of Independence is blank, though. On the back of the document, you can see the upside-down words "Original Declaration of Independence dated 4th July 1776." There's nothing secret about that message!

## EXPLORE MORE!

IT MAY NOT HAVE A SECRET MAP, BUT THE DECLARATION OF INDEPENDENCE DOES HAVE A MYSTERY MARK ON IT. A CLOSE LOOK SHOWS A HANDPRINT ON THE FRONT OF THE DOCUMENT. NO ONE KNOWS WHOSE IT IS. BUT IT'S NOT FROM A FOUNDING FATHER. IT APPEARED IN THE EARLY 1900s.

This photo shows a copy of the engrossed Declaration of Independence. The original is kept at the National Archives in Washington, DC.

# PARTY IN THE COLONIES

The people who approved the Declaration of Independence knew that July 4 was a big day for the country. You might think there was a huge celebration on the original Independence Day. This was not the case.

While the colonists did celebrate the Declaration of Independence, they didn't all celebrate the day it was adopted. News didn't travel fast back then. It took time for the colonists to learn what happened on July 4. For example, on July 8, a celebration and reading of the declaration took place in Philadelphia. But it took nearly a month for the document to reach the people of South Carolina.

### EXPLORE MORE!

BEFORE THEY BROKE AWAY FROM GREAT BRITAIN, COLONISTS HELD BIG CELEBRATIONS FOR BRITISH KING GEORGE'S BIRTHDAY. BUT IN THE SUMMER OF 1776, SOME COLONISTS HELD PRETEND **FUNERALS** FOR THE KING. THIS WAS THEIR WAY OF SHOWING THAT HE NO LONGER HAD A HOLD OVER THEM.

Colonists pull down a statue of King George III after the Declaration of Independence is approved.

# THE KING AND THE DIARY

On July 4, 1776, the colonists made it clear that they were not happy with King George. What was his response? For years, a story said that he wrote in his diary that day, "Nothing of importance happened today." However, King George didn't even keep a diary.

The false story likely came from a true one about another ruler. King Louis XVI of France wrote in his diary that nothing happened on July 14, 1789. This was the day French citizens captured a Paris fortress and prison and started their own fight for independence.

## EXPLORE MORE!

LEADERS IN GREAT BRITAIN, INCLUDING THE KING, PROBABLY DID NOT GET A LOOK AT THE DECLARATION OF INDEPENDENCE UNTIL MORE THAN A MONTH AFTER IT WAS APPROVED. IT WOULD HAVE TAKEN ABOUT FIVE WEEKS FOR A COPY OF THE DOCUMENT TO BE SENT ACROSS THE ATLANTIC OCEAN.

# THE SOUND OF FREEDOM

The Liberty Bell in Philadelphia is probably best known for the large crack in its side. One story about how the crack got there says that it happened while the bell was ringing in celebration on July 4, 1776. It's a good story, but it's not true. The bell probably didn't ring that day at all.

The Liberty Bell's original name was the State House Bell. It was renamed in honor of the antislavery movement in the 1800s.

The Liberty Bell actually cracked twice. The first time was probably just after it was made in the 1750s. It was recast, or made again, after that. The crack we see in the bell today likely happened in the 1840s.

# Explore More!

IF YOU WANT TO VISIT THE LIBERTY BELL IN PHILADELPHIA, DON'T EXPECT TO HEAR IT RING. SOMETIME AFTER THE FAMOUS CRACK APPEARED, ANOTHER ONE WEAKENED THE BELL EVEN MORE. THE BELL HAS NOT RUNG SINCE THEN. NO ONE HAS HEARD THE SOUND OF THE LIBERTY BELL SINCE 1846.

# AMERICA CELEBRATES

Today, the Fourth of July is a national holiday. Schools, businesses, and banks are closed so people can celebrate America's freedom. But this was not always the case. It took almost 100 years for the date to become a national holiday.

Even though Americans had always marked Independence Day, celebrations became more common in the United States after the War of 1812. This was another war between the United States and Great Britain. Finally, in 1870, Congress passed a law to make Independence Day a federal, or national, holiday.

## EXPLORE MORE!

A FEW LUCKY PEOPLE HAVE A SPECIAL FOURTH OF JULY CELEBRATION EACH YEAR. CHILDREN WHO HAVE A FAMILY CONNECTION TO SIGNERS OF THE DECLARATION OF INDEPENDENCE TAP THE LIBERTY BELL 13 TIMES, ONE FOR EACH ORIGINAL COLONY. MANY OTHER BELLS RING AROUND PHILADELPHIA AT THE SAME TIME.

People wave flags as they watch an Independence Day parade.

# FRIENDS AND FOES

Thomas Jefferson and John Adams were both important Founding Fathers. They worked closely together for many years. However, they often argued about how the new country should be formed. At one point, they stopped speaking to each other for 12 years. As they got older, though, they put their differences aside.

JOHN ADAMS

Adams once wrote to Jefferson, "You and I ought not to die before we have explained ourselves to each other."

Jefferson and Adams both died on July 4, 1826, the 50th anniversary of the adoption of the Declaration of Independence. It's a common belief that Adams whispered, "Jefferson survives," before he died. However, there's no proof this happened. Jefferson actually died a few hours before Adams.

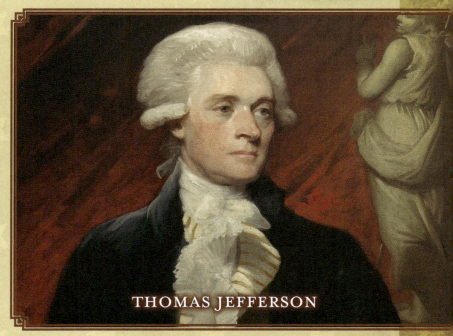

THOMAS JEFFERSON

## EXPLORE MORE!

JEFFERSON AND ADAMS WERE NOT THE ONLY PRESIDENTS WHO DIED ON INDEPENDENCE DAY. JAMES MONROE, THE FIFTH PRESIDENT AND A FOUNDING FATHER, DIED ON JULY 4, 1831. OF THE FIRST FIVE AMERICAN PRESIDENTS, THREE DIED ON THE FOURTH OF JULY.

# OUR TRUE HISTORY

The creation of the Declaration of Independence was a huge event in American history. But did you know that some of the most important ideas in the document come from the same country the colonists were fighting? Thomas Jefferson borrowed ideas about equality and people's rights from British writers.

American history is full of interesting facts and stories. Sometimes you need to dig deep to find out the truth about an event or a person. You can do this by reading and asking lots of questions. You'll probably make some interesting discoveries.

## Explore More

THE PRACTICE OF SHOOTING OFF FIREWORKS STARTED LONG BEFORE AMERICA'S FIRST INDEPENDENCE DAY. THE CHINESE USED FIREWORKS AS EARLY AS 200 BCE. BUT THEY DIDN'T LOOK LIKE THE COLORFUL ONES WE SEE TODAY ON THE FOURTH OF JULY. UNTIL THE 1830S, FIREWORKS WERE ALL ORANGE.

The date of Independence Day may not be as important as the American spirit that it celebrates.

# GLOSSARY

**American Revolution:** The war in which the colonies won their freedom from England.

**approve:** To give official agreement.

**celebrate:** To honor with special activities.

**declaration:** A document that contains an official statement.

**delegate:** A representative of one of the 13 colonies.

**document:** A formal piece of writing.

**draft:** A document before completion.

**engross:** To prepare an official document in large, clear writing.

**formal:** Following an established form.

**funeral:** A ceremony to mark the burial of the dead.

**inspire:** To cause someone to want to do something.

**proposal:** Something that is presented to a person or group of people to consider.

# FOR MORE INFORMATION

## BOOKS
Black, Sonia. *Thomas Jefferson: Man of the People*. New York, NY: Children's Press, 2020.

Clay, Kathryn. *The Declaration of Independence: Introducing Primary Sources*. North Mankato, MN: Capstone Press, 2017.

Kaul, Jennifer. *The American Colonies: Asking Tough Questions*. North Mankato, MN: Capstone Press, 2017.

## WEBSITES

**DK Find Out! American Revolution**
www.dkfindout.com/us/history/american-revolution/
Discover more about the people and events at the center of America's fight for freedom.

**Ducksters: Independence Day**
www.ducksters.com/holidays/independence_day.php
Learn more fun facts about America's holiday.

**Thomas Jefferson: The Declaration of Independence**
www.americaslibrary.gov/aa/jefferson/aa_jefferson_declar_3.html
Find out more about the document we celebrate on Independence Day.

**Publisher's note to educators and parents:** Our editors have carefully reviewed these websites to ensure that they are suitable for students. Many websites change frequently, however, and we cannot guarantee that a site's future contents will continue to meet our high standards of quality and educational value. Be advised that students should be closely supervised whenever they access the internet.

# INDEX

Adams, John, 8, 9, 26, 27

Continental Congress, 6, 8, 10, 11, 12, 15

Declaration of Independence, 4, 6, 8, 9, 10, 11, 12, 13, 14, 15, 16, 17, 18, 19, 20, 24, 26, 28

fireworks, 4, 28

Founding Fathers, 4, 26, 27

Fourth of July, 4, 24, 28

Franklin, Benjamin, 8

Great Britain, 6, 18, 20, 21, 24

Hancock, John, 14, 15

Jefferson, Thomas, 8, 11, 26, 27, 28

King George III, 6, 18, 19, 20, 21

King Louis XVI, 20

Lexington, Massachusetts, 15

Liberty Bell, 22, 23, 24

Monroe, James, 27

Philadelphia, Pennsylvania, 13, 18, 22, 23, 24

13 colonies, 5, 6, 7

Washington, George, 10, 14, 15